# VANDEMONIAN

Previous poetry collections include:

*Wake* (Flarestack Poets, 2009)
*Trans* (The Collective Press, Wales, 2005)

To Rowan
with best
wishes

# VANDEMONIAN
## Cliff Forshaw

PUBLICATIONS
2013

Published by Arc Publications
Nanholme Mill, Shaw Wood Road
Todmorden OL14 6DA, UK
www.arcpublications.co.uk

Design by Tony Ward
Printed in Great Britain by TJ International,
Padstow, Cornwall

978 1904614 60 9 (pbk)
978 1904614 72 2 (hbk)

ACKNOWLEDGEMENTS

Some of these poems first appeared in the following publications:
*The Common* (USA); *Famous Reporter* (Australia); *Light on Don Bank: Fifteen Years of Live Poets* eds. Danny Gardner and Sue Hicks (Sydney: Live Poets' Press, 2006); *Mood Lightning* ed. Ten Ch'in Û (Sydney: Imaginal Press, 2004); *Poetry Wales*; *Sketches, Dispatches, Hull Tales and Ballads* (Kingston Press, 2012); *Tales of the Fox*, CD (Trinity and All Saints College, Leeds, 2006). An earlier version of the sequence 'Tiger' appeared as a chapbook (HappenStance, 2011). The sequence *A Ned Kelly Hymnal* appeared as a chapbook (A Paper Special Edition / Cherry on the Top Press, 2008). The Ned Kelly, Trucanini and William Lanne poems appeared as illustrated sequences on the web journal *Enter Text* 7.2 'Human Rights, Human Wrongs' (Brunel University, 2007); 'Loop' appeared as a Carol Rumens Poem of the Week on *The Guardian* website.

The author would like to thank Joe Bugden and the Tasmanian Writers' Centre, Hobart, for their hospitality during his very fruitful period as International Writer in Residence. He owes many of these poems to their Island of Residencies scheme. He would also like to thank Les Wicks, a great host on the mainland.

Cover image:
Detail from 'The Conciliation' (1840) by Benjamin Duttereau by kind permission of the Tasmanian Museum and Art Gallery.

**Editor for the UK & Ireland: John W. Clarke**

*for Mary*

# Contents

# VANDEMONIAN

# Landfall in Abel's Garden

… and the Dreaming dreamed itself an island
in the shape of the human heart:
an unmoored rock, but fertile,
drifting way off from mainland
while wind and rain dissolved its shores.

And mists hung about its beaches,
caught themselves in trees, straggled
branches, blurring upland reaches.
Elsewhere shrugged itself to driftwood,
fetched up, half-worked, sea-wrack.

And this Dreaming dreamed itself *Trowenna*;
seems it dreamed and stranded
clumps of its people on this island:
few in shy groups tending
small fires on its fringes,
slowly raising middens
of shellfish from the sea.

\*

From Batavia, Antony Van Diemen,
of the *Dutch East India C°*,
summoned skippers, two skeely seamen,
unfurled the map of white, said "Go!"

Down there was Unknown, lacking features:
*Terra Australis Incognita*
– who knew what riches, what savage creatures…?

Happens Abel Tasman made first landfall,
– a lonely flag on a spit of sand –
baptised this place *Van Diemen's Land*.

And when it came to start again,
forget the past, *that convict stain,*
(those Vandemonian *marks of Cain*),

it seemed appropriate, somehow right
to take Abel's as its given name:
*O Tasmania,* my Refoundland.

*[Rebaptised, perhaps too soon;
though lucky landfall had not fallen
to Van Dieman's other skipper,
who went by the handle of the mouthful,
Ide Tjerscxzoon.]*

\*

Others came to tame this land
and turned it to a cage:
with bars of sea and sand,
and walls of mountain range.

*[The old maps on the wall
mark Devon, Dorset, Kent:
named less for home than regiments.]*

And the wildlife is renamed
Hyena, Tiger, Devil.
Oh, we will make a garden
of this savage plot.

Blue gums, silver wattle, cycads;
pademelons hopping across wet tracks.

Oh, we will name new worlds
on the template of the old.
Have gardens of lily, rose,
forests of myrtle, oak.

\*

Now the snake in every garden snores,
it's the little lamb which can't lie down...

*Bountiful, bountiful.*
The Lamb has placed a bounty
on every Tiger's head;
many happy returns
to the smooth hunter who
gets to sell its skin
for waistcoats, gloves.

The Lord is our Shepherd
and we remain His sheep.

[*"The Superintendent of the
Hampshire and Surrey Hills
Establishments is authorised to
give the following rewards for the
destruction of noxious animals
in those districts. For every Male
Hyena 5/-. For every Female with
or without young 7/-. Half the above
prices for Male and Female devils
and Wild Dogs. When 20 hyenas
have been destroyed the reward for
the next 20 will be increased to 6/-
and 8/- respectively and afterward
an additional 1/- per head will be
made after every seven killed until
the reward makes 10/- for every male
and 12/- for every female."* Edward
Curr, Chief Resident, Van Dieman's
Land Company, 1830.]

## Lat. 43º

On an island off an island,
land hangs from land
by a rope of sand:
this epitome of peninsula,
the penal colony's
penal colony's
penal colony.

[*The colony's sad tale:*
*this is where it all hangs out,*
*daggy as shitballed sheep.*]

Here even *Terra Nullius*
tails off into *Nowhere.*
And to say, of course, it's *nullius*
is to say that they're No-One:
shy figures, wallflowers,
shadows of unhandy men
immured in the Garden of Diemen.

Nothing between here and the Southern Pole.
Nothing to stop waves from far west
as Cape Town get up some speed,
build walls, build ever-higher seas.
And just where is *here* when here
is constantly swept past?
*Roaring Forties.*

*The very day we landed upon the fatal shore,*
*The planters they stood around us, full twenty score or more;*
*They ranked us up like horses and sold us out of hand,*
*They roped us to the plough, brave boys, to plough Van Diemen's Land.*

# The Man

Arthur looked right into the heart
of Van Diemen's Land,
saw sour evil there.

Mission from God.
See vice, depravity,
get venal details recorded:
decide Black Books,
leather-bound, three foot high.

Bureaucrat of punishment,
mechanic of the soul's hard grind;
makes damn sure they work
in the teeth of unrelenting cogs,
do their clockwork time.

God's mills. Else feel
that huge fly-wheel
wipe the smirk right off
the shirker's face;
rearrange the fate
of any larrikin bloke
who don't adjust
to the rhythm of Justice,
submit to the enlightened rigour
of its damn close mesh.

*

The Governor built his prisons,
but he built his chapels, too.
Now the Lamb of God beams down
in light that's brightly stained,
right foreleg implausibly curled

around a regimental flag.
Cloisters bristle with pennants,
improbably unfurled,
stiffened with gold wind,
backbones of wire.

Elsewhere, another chapel where
Irishmen of much conviction
stutter prayers to a shiny Virgin;
paint chipped from a toenail,
as a sandalled foot
arches over a snake's head
– crushes that twisty dead-beat
in the lime-green grass. *Psst. Psst.*
See where fingers touched those feet,
where dusty plaster falls away like cake?

# Black Line

They trawled the island: think *dragnet*.
Sought strange dwellers. Perhaps
Calibans, half-man, half-fish?
A witch's bastard offspring,
runs dropped by Sycorax?
Netted few; inept, thank Christ!
(Two to be precise. Young boy, old man.
The rest melted into rivers, trees.)

*[2,200 men: 550 troops, 700 convicts,*
*the rest free settlers; 1,000 muskets,*
*30,000 rounds of ammunition;*
*300 pairs of handcuffs.]*

They'll be back with new ways
to chase the Blackfella off,
or pen him up down there, paddocked
on that out-of-the-way peninsula.
Make this place safe
for Albion's sinners and her sheep.

17

# The Dog Line

At Eaglehawk Neck Bay,
not quite one hundred yards
of windscoured shell-grit, scrub,
keep estuary from the Southern Ocean,
and this far south,
that's some rough old sea.

Oil lamps shed light
on shattered cockleshells.
Now night has a frontier:
a screen glows white enough
to catch fugitive shadows.
Got it covered,
pinned down every smell.

["Whether Port Arthur is an
'Earthly Hell' or not, it has at all
events its Cerberus… Their dogs
form an unpassable line."
T.J. Lemprière.]

Dog-lurch. Claw-barrel.
Moon-snarl. Chain-strain.
Insects, beam-caught.
Dribble. Spatter. Flea-scratch.
Scatter cockleshells.

Ground to dust. Dog-weight.
Sniff piss-reek.
Snuffle odd spot-shine.
Slaver trails as moon
skids slowly past each post.

["Those out-of-the-way pretend-
ers to dogship […] rejoiced in
such soubriquets as Caesar,
Pompey, Ajax, Achilles, Ugly
Mug, Jowler, Tear'em, Muzzle
'em […] There were the black,
the white, the brindle, the grey
and the grisly, the rough and the
smooth, the crop-eared and the
lop-eared, the gaunt and the grim.
Every four-footed, black-fanged
individual among them would
have taken first prize in his own
class for ugliness and ferocity at
any show."
Harden S. Melville, 1837.]

More dogs! More dogs!
They paw the platform's edge.
Further posts reared up from sea.
Southern Finisterre:
something cuts the churn beyond.
Rumour is, guards straight out the slaughterhouse
dump stinking tripes.
The gleeful Watch as pink skeins grey,

18

knifed from below that slice of moon:
off-shore, beyond the dogs,
secured, they say, by sharks.

Along the shore,
            across the bay:
                        semaphore.

What's happened down
in Port Arthur's known
in minutes;
half-an-hour
and it's whispered up
in Hobart Town.

One convict, William Hunt
(former actor, ex "strolling mountebank"),
hopped it,
disguised as a buck kangaroo.

I guess he sewed himself
into that big boomer's skin.
His disguise *too* good.
Two guards, doubtless thinking *meat*,
pursued, levelled muskets at the beast.

At one bound he's just another hunted roo.
Guards ("We'll have that cunt!")
stop, confused as the big bouncer croaks:
"Don't shoot! Don't shoot!
I'm only Billy Hunt."

# Dumb Cells

They shut your trap. The warder said nowt,
bundled you – poor bugger! – into dark.
This monkhood turns grasses Trappist:
*dumb cells*, down there no light, no noise, no talk.

Without the light, it's all bad dreams, blind faith.
You touch the wall to feel the world's still there.
For days you wheel over landless seas.
You pray for Sunday: clanks, chains, the key.

But now, felt slippers, the guards' steps muffled,
you're hooded with a *beak*, prodded, shuffled
(damp-smells, echoes) towards a sniff of sun,
air, black on the back of your neck and hands.

*Sunday*, each man in his privy wooden stall,
you take your only communion in the swell
of hymns. Each soul can shout himself out
from his little wedge of God-pointed dark.

You sing your name: it fills your throat, your mouth;
not sure what is echo, what is prayer;
once more you're wheeling over what brought you here:
*Roaring Forties*, that ache of nothing to the south.

# Bird

You work. Pick oakum in solitude.
In the yard you're hidden by a mask
that twists each jail-bird's face into beak.

Nothing to say or do, but *Work is Prayer*.
You do your bird. You do your time. Keep shtum
Keep nose clean. Keep hands to yourself. Keep mum.

One day in the yard, a man runs head-first, mad
against the wall. Falls, gets up, head-butts
his way, almost *through* brick: again and again,
you hear skin and bone on stone. That crack.

It echoes down the months. It fills your cell.
Your mind's eye colonised by the twitch
of a wounded bird, the way it fell;
how blood frothed cobbles, sun smirked along its beak.

# Suddenly One Sunday
*Port Arthur, 28 April 1996*


Suddenly one Sunday
a man goes into the Broad Arrow Café,
hands out the punishment to all and sundry.

Full of tourists. Bad timing, very tough luck –
to coincide with some long-simmered grudge
and a semi-automatic. Faster than *Shit! Fuck!*

The newly articulate rhetoric of an AR-15
making its incontrovertible points with thirty
rounds of well-considered disputation in each magazine,

pressing home the argument with a leg or shoulder.
*Quiet lad, bit of a loner.*
Back of neck, spine; exiting splinters of bone.

The chorus to that song keeps growing longer:
*Columbine, Virgina Tech, San Ysidro, Aramoana,
Hungerford, Dunblane, Killeen, Fort Hood, Utøya.*

A number you can't get out of your head.
Eighteen wounded, thirty-five dead.

# Trucanini
*Last full-blood Tasmanian Aborigine (1812?-1876)*


Trucanini, Truganner, I'm not sure what to call you,
your name has grown vague and lost as *Trowenna*.

Trucanini, Truganner, last full-blood born here,
raped by whitefella convicts, sterile with gonorrhoea.

Trucanini, Truganner, still hanging round their woodsmoke,
you sell yourself to sealers for a handful of tea or sugar.

Trucanini, Truganner, they murdered your mother;
come again, a little later, killed your new step-mother.

Trucanini, Truganner, whitemen murdered your intended,
convict mutineers stole your blood-sister Moorina.

Trucanini, Truganner, there'll soon be no one left now,
so many sold to slavers just like your tribal sisters.

Comes another whiteman: comes George Augustus Robinson,
together with Wooraddy, loyal guide and his Good Friday.

This whitefella Robinson's a missionary unlike any other:
cockney builder become explorer, *The Great Conciliator*.

Trucanini, Truganner, help-meet and translator:
interpret, make word-lists, catalogue their customs.

Trucanini, Truganner – tiny, tiny, tiny –
married Wooraddy, also full-blood out of Bruny.

Trucanini, Truganner, with Robinson you both wander,
so long since you left your home on Bruny Island.

You go gathering them in now, most-trusted Trucanini.
Orphan-mother to the whitefella's blackface piccaninny.

Interpreter, translator, Truganner, Trucanini,
in your story I hear echoes of Pocahontas, La Malinche.

*Traduttori sono traditori*: I heard an Italian say in Sydney.
And, for a long time, I thought, Trucanini, Truganner,
how lives fork when we live in a stranger's tongue.

*My Lord's a Cockney Shepherd*
*who's bringing in His Flock*
*and we're singing Ba Ba Black Sheep*
*as we huddle in His Fold.*

*Some say I'm rounding up the black sheep,*
*like the shepherd's faithful dog,*
*but there's nothing left but pasture,*
*and my forest's turned to logs.*

*Now there's a bounty on the Tiger,*
*there's a fence across the land,*
*and they're grazing fluffy white sheep*
*while the Shepherd sings the hymns.*

*He leads us to the Promised Land*
*where we will all be safe,*
*and our Pen is Flinders Island,*
*though there's not many still alive.*

*But the Master's gone and left us,*
*least what was left of that last Fold.*
*Shipped us back from Flinders Island*
*to slums and rum in Oyster Cove.*

Trucanini, Truganner, now you're dying on your own,
the doctors pick your bones like ghostly thylacines.

Trucanini, Truganner, your flesh and blood all gone,
your people dead as Dodos and they've stolen what remains,

You star in that *National Picture* high up on the Museum wall,
but though your bones are still raked in a big glass case,
    you saved *No One* after all.

# The Ballad of William Lanne
### Or, "The Blackfella's Skeleton"

Now there's a funny kind of Ballad,
Penned by your Boneyard Bards,
Of what happened down in Hobart
When the Surgeons came to Town.

*The Coroner's Paper's white as Bone*
*And the Ink's as black as Skin*
*And the Seal upon the Parchment's*
*Red as Blood, but not so thin.*

Trucanini's final Husband,
A Bloke called Billy Lanne,
Died in 1869,
The last Full-Blood Tassie Man.

If this was *Terra Nullius,*
Then William was No-One.
No Diggers could ever count or name
All the Species that are gone.

Old Darwin, when he studied
Where Nature had gone wrong,
Found Dead-Ends merely croaked
And sang no great Swan-Song.

But the Dinosaurs have left
Fossilized Rosetta Stones,
So the Doctors licked their Chops
At the thought of Billy's Bones.

One Night old Saw-Bones Crowther
Sneaked on Tip-Toes to the Morgue;
The Lamplight glints on his Case of Knives
Beside that laid-out Corpse.

26

Now the Surgeon's filthy Cuffs
Are rolled back for Steel & Skill:
His Scalpel skims the Cadaver's Scalp,
Peels back that sad black Skin.

Now William's Face falls like a Mask
– Crestfallen, sloughed-off Skin –
As Crowther teases out the Skull
And slips a White Bloke's in.

Now a new Head fills that Death Mask,
Sewn into the Blackfella's Grin;
The Bastard wraps the Brain-Pain up
In a Piece of old Sealskin.

He'll send it off to London
To the Royal bloody Surgeons there,
So he tip-toes from the Morgue,
Sniffs Reward in the dawn-fresh Air.

Skullduggery's soon discovered
(*reports our Hobart hack*):
Examining Our Cadaver's Head,
"The Face turned round," the M.O. said
and this new Saw-Bones "saw Bones
were sticking out the Back."

So, to stop the Pommie Surgeons,
Getting their bloody filthy Hands
On the Rest of that last Tasmanian

they chopped off its Feet,
        and they chopped off its Hands,
                and they slung them in the Dunny.

The Cadaver was buried,
But secretly next Night
Royal Society Gentlemen
Dug it up by their Lamplight.

Time waits for no Tasmanian:
The Quick must be quick with the Dead.
They dissected William's Skeleton
(*sans Feet, sans Hands, sans Head*).

Did grave Doctors cast their Lots
To perform their Funeral Rites?
They cut away Black Flesh that rots,
Redeemed the White Bone into Light.

Meanwhile, bobbing off to London,
Seal-Skin begins to stink.
Sailors got shot of it Overboard,
Flung Billy's Skull in the Drink.

It's a very sorry end,
To what became of William Lanne:
      The butchers lost his feet and hands,
          His head went bobbing far from land
– Do you think one day they'll find those bones?
      Will his skull wash up on Tassie's sands?
        Can he be buried whole again?

... *Yeah, yeah,*
        *but from Darwin down to Melbourne,*
          *the learned doctors said:*
        *"Let the weak fall by the wayside,*
          *for the strong live off the dead.*

*To stay alive is to survive*
  *against the bleakest odds.*
*Embrace your Fate. Know your Place.*
  *Accept the Will of God.*

*His cards were always marked,*
  *just like the thylacine's:*
*inevitable extinction's*
  *written into defunct genes."*


Course, it's a sad, sad end, this dead dead-end,
    but, when all is said and done,
can't stand in the way of Progress
    – Thank Christ they're bleedin' gawn.

We gave them a good shake,
    but they just could not wake,
        the Dreamtime had crusted their eyes.

So we left them for dead,
    and strode on ahead,
        and were blessed with this golden sunrise.

Our shadows are shortening behind us.
    Our dead are all dead and all gone.
They couldn't come with us, they couldn't adapt,
    their bones lie bleached by the sun.

It's dawn in the Lucky Country
    and it's time, it's time to move on.
Let the women and the crocs shed tears,
        these fellas had been just hanging on
            these last four thousand years.

Long time dreamed of falling,
	Down through seaweed, silver shoal.
Up above the light was fading,
	Waves tumbled, roiled and boiled.

Night presses down so heavy.
	Down here's just salty sea-bed.
Empty sockets see nothing, nothing.
	I need eyes like I need holes in my head.

Teeth shiver-shiver my jaw.
	No flesh left to pad them all in.
The world has ripped up all its Laws,
	Left us dismembered,
	Dismembered and bearing white grins.

## Funeral Rites

*"Don't let them cut me, but bury me behind the mountains."*
TRUCANINI'S LAST WORDS.

I BODY

The Museum wants my body.
Don't let them cut me, please.
Maybe bury me behind big mountains
where unseen rivers flow down to the sea.

Or wrap me in a canvas bag,
with a stone to weight my feet.
Somewhere off Bruny Island,
please drop me good and deep.

Given half a chance, I think I still
could find some kind of peace
in the bone-chill of the Channel
where the water's dark and deep.

Take a little boat to row me out,
slip me overboard, let me go,
let me swirl in the currents
of the D'Entrecasteaux.

Let me sink, just let me go,
like my sisters and all my men,
like some quiet, best undiscovered,
spirit of that Channel's deepest part.

Now you're Queen Trucanini
and you're keeping lonely court,
crowned only by the whitefolk
of growing Hobart Town.

Trucanini, Trucanini, fearful of spirits;
Rowra's revenge for tribes long betrayed.
"Missus, Rowra catch me. Rowra catch me."
Come coma days. Come drowning dreams.
Come ghosts. Come bad memory stuff
of sealers and Flinders and wretched Oyster Cove.

Come Woorady. Come Moorina.
Come all tribal sisters.
Come Mama. Come Step-Mama.
Come all that is known.

*Missus, Rowra catchme. Catchme. Catchme.*
*Missus, Rowra catchme. Catchme in dreams.*
Come Robinson. Come doctors.
Come William's scattered bones.
"Don't let them cut me!
Don't let them cut me, please!"

Come words. Come silence.
Come whisper. Come scream.

III 11 MAY 1876

Crowned *Queen of Aborigines*
      when you had no people left,
*le tout* Hobart's out to see
      the Governor pay respects
to you, the great dead dignitary
      of some awful far-off place.

As they watched your little coffin
      borne through mourning crowds,
few knew or could suspect
      the emptiness that bobbed
in that child-sized snuffed-out box.

Not behind mountains,
      nor sinking through water;
not in this coffin,
      your body's elsewhere.

[Taken, your tiny remains,
stashed them in a vault.
Hush your bones
in the Protestant's cool Chapel.
Keep that secret shushed,
deep behind the Penitentiary's tall walls.]

## IV THE NATIONAL PICTURE

I was dug up two years later,
with my skin and fat flensed off,
and my bones were boiled and nailed
into an apple crate.

Once more left forgotten,
I'm in another dusty box.
Enough kinfolks' bones down here to make
the Museum our family vault.

Upstairs in the Gallery,
I'm in that big "National Picture".
That's life, though there I'm larger by far:
all eyes drawn to me, its dark star,

bringing all my people in
to George Augustus Robinson,
*The Conciliator* (our lost Messiah),
in his important coat and hat.

I puzzle why, at our feet,
the artist's strangely painted
the wallaby in peace
with his kinsman's kangaroo hounds.

## V RESTRUNG

Decades later,
they stumbled on my crate.
Put me together,
restrung my bones.

Hung me upstairs
in a glass-fronted case.
Faces came, went,
breathed on the glass.

Came one day, again
they rattled me down,
for another thirty years
in the cellar's winter-dark.

'76. Could have celebrated
one hundred years of waking up dead.

Called it Centenary, had me *cremated*.
All those years since my lying in state.

Smoke, and getting scattered:
I'm down to dust and ashes,

grit pitting the waters
of the D'Entrecasteaux.

Out there, the surf explodes,
dawn's firing up Storm Bay.

Once in the Channel, you hope,
but never really know just when you're safely through

and going somewhere that looks
just a little like you could maybe call it home.

## REINCARNATED LIGHT

*The thylacine, or "Tasmanian tiger", the world's largest marsupial carnivore, originally native to continental Australia, Tasmania and New Guinea, was declared extinct in 1986. Though deliberately hunted to the brink of extinction throughout the nineteenth and early twentieth century, it was given the status of protected species two months before the last documented tiger died in 1936 in a Hobart zoo.*

*Attempts to clone the thylacine, using DNA from preserved specimens, have so far proved unsuccessful. The tiger has assumed a popular mythic status in Tasmania, with unconfirmed sightings continuing to this day.*

# Tiger

LOOP
*62 seconds of the extinct thylacine on film.*

Within the box, it growls, it twists,
scowls through its repertoire of tricks,
ignores the camera – or gurns up close, turns
again, to flop, to gnaw that paw-trapped bone.

It paces out its trap of light; one hundred reps
while hindquarters zither bars of sun;
claws cage's mesh, hangs stretched
as if to take the measure of itself.

You saw. You see. And what we've got is what was shot:
short clips, fragments caught and stitched
together in a loop of black and white.

Nine lives? Not quite. It's down. It's out.
It's on its feet and born again. Like a repetition
compulsion, like… like reincarnated light.

*Tarraleah… Wayatinah…*

Extinct, this creature's everywhere
from CD sleeves to bottled beer.
With trademark stripes, it zebras out
between the gums' abstracted light.
They've even tigered my hired Mazda's plate.
Everything's branded. *Tasmania – your natural state.*

Now you see them. Now they're gone.
Did this tiger's go-faster stripes
aid recognition in the loping pack?

Eucalypts, eucalypts at speed,
late sun flickers through those trees:
at the tarmac's edge, off-cuts of fur, strange weeds.

Billboards, stores along the newly-metalled road:
ironic ads, that hide's barcode.

*... Catagunya, Lake Repulse...*

## OLD HAIRY

And here he is, "Old Hairy",
red and skinny, tough as boots,
four thousand years old if he's a day;
forever flat out and in pursuit

of… whatever. The chase goes on and on.
That endless prey's his last: the one
that's slipped its skeleton through a crack in stone;
a white shadow in the rock that's worn him down
to skin and bone. That's skin? That's bone?

(To the south, earth shifts, Tassie breaks free:
distant cousins in cold high woods, cut off by sea.)

Dry as parchment, brittle as sticks:
*mummified mainland thylacine,*
*found base of shaft, Nullarbor Plain, '66.*

*… Zeehan, Strahan, Teepookana…*

41

QUIRK

Next to extinct stripes, the stuttered screen:
one skull, one larger skeleton, a box
of assorted bones and one small stuffed thylacine.

Crouched here, what looks foetal, but's been marked
in ink: *Pouch young – before 1910,*
almost hairless, pickled in a jar.
You think of what this means, then look again.

Closer, where that curiously upturned snout
sniffs at its bung of dead trapped air,
a few surprisingly wiry bristles sprout,
magnified by the glass's curve.

Above the brownish bevel, the century's dripped white.
Eyes closed, it noses out the hang of things. Just what
has pierced that lid with long thin fangs? Stalactites.


*… Marakoopa, Crotty Dam…*

*Pouch Young.* But that familiar foetal curve
keeps on deceiving right down to this tail's curl.
No stripes. It's just a flourish underlining
the space that's signally left unsigned. No god
has scratched his mark. Here's work-in-progress still.

*Marsupium,* meaning "pouch", much like the Greek
*Thylakos,* ditto one in leather. What light gets in
stains it brown as old veneer;
what you've got's gone Dutch with death. Still-life.
I'm thinking *nature morte*: a flitch of bacon,
hung pheasant, hare, a jug of flattening beer,

when I see quicksilvered against what's aborted, jarred,
my reflection caught upon that quirk,
light from that screen turning us all to silent stars.

*... Lileah, Nabageena...*

What *is* this stuff with tails? This slump of fur
that mimes the body's weight, intimates
the slow tug of earth that gets us all. You swerve
to miss these weird speed bumps, glimpse
a forested ridge in the marginalia of the road,
a premonition of mountains in that spine's hump.

Each is a map to what still lies, lies still
– yet moves – now like a wave, now flat-out:
roadstone's quake, asphalt fever, that tremor
shivering towards you through the heat-haze,
visions of angels skating on the shimmer.

Blind bend. Horn. The dopplered blare
through ears and car and ribs. Road train.
Chained logs, knee-trembled, hovering on compressed air.


*... Savage River, Blackguard's Hill...*

IN INVERTED COMMAS

Others are Disney-flat, out-run cartoons
who've failed to burrow into tarmac,
who've found it far too hard, too black.
At this one's mouth, a speech-balloon
where asphalt's slick and almost pink,
as if someone's scrubbed long and hard at red
daubed words, the rumour's near indelible ink.

Haunches, muddied pelts, dithered paws,
little fangs gnawing on the camber;
snouts punctuated by inverted commas of claws:
irony or speech marks, a question mark of tail,
rising like the intonation you get round here.

So *politely* put. But a question nonetheless.
Demands sometime, sometime quite soon, you answer, "Yes.".


… *Cradle Mountain, Pieman River…*

POSSUM

Now something's listening out for the *ute*'s hissed tread.
Forests. The further in, the more you get.
Possums, not playing at it, they're really dead.
Now that the Tassie tiger's gone, the devils
are in league with *us*. Plastinated Penguin
(pub. lib. & overdue) says: *Thylacine males,*
*like Tas. devils (their closest extant relatives),*
*had pseudo-pouches to protect their testicles.*

The rumour's going round (you heard it here
from those who heard it first) that once you've done
your stretch you're out of here. *They lie in wait.*
Inside time, we also serve who only...
*The truth's out there.* It's on the outside's where
you'll need all the balls you think that you, your family, got.

... *Misery Plateau, Gates of Hell...*

46

## THE BOTTOM LINE

*Tarraleah, Wayatinah, Catagunya, Lake Repulse,*
*Zeehan, Strahan, Teepookana, Marakoopa, Crotty Dam,*
*Lileah, Nabageena, Savage River, Blackguard's Hill.*
*Out of Queenstown, down the Franklin,*
*at Cradle Mountain, the Walls of Jerusalem;*
*one on the banks of Pieman River,*
*past the place they named Corinna;*
*unconfirmed sightings at Misery Plateau, Gates of Hell.*

On the road to Wayatinah,
hard to tell in scratchy rain
if what stripes dusk's a mangy
dog, its ribs all chiaroscuro hunger,
or weather rubbing landscape out.

Or, the passing place, where headlights catch
what crosses track – that flash glimpsed in the paddock,
head down low, salaamed to dirt:
bowing or praying. What you see at first
is resolved, from something grumbling an argument
with the earth itself, to some long-snouted thing
with life between its teeth, its dragged-back iffy twitch.

For days, that nervous stuff all looks like prey:
a lope that's dopplered through the boles of trees,
is *there… there… there,* is disappeared.
And all around, the bottom line goes:
*Tarraleah, Wayatinah, Catagunya…*

Past the place they named Corinna,
what you hear is ghosts, ghosts, ghosts…

THYLACINUS CYNOCEPHALUS

*"Caught kangaroo and killed one hyaena on the sandy
beach. The hyaena is called mannalargenna (east
coast), cabbarone-nenner, by the Cape Grim, lowenin,
by Jenny (north coast) clinner, by the Cape Portland
warternoonner, by the Brune cannenner, and by the
Oyster Bay lartner..."*

GEORGE AUGUSTUS ROBINSON
diary entry, 30 August 1833

Zebra Opossum. Zebra Wolf.
Tasmanian Zebra. Marsupial Wolf.
Striped Wolf. Tiger Wolf. Tasmanian Wolf.
*Lagunta, corinna, laoonana, ka-nunnah*

Van Diemen's Land Tiger. Tasmanian Tiger.
Bulldog Tiger. Greyhound Tiger.
Hyaena. Native Hyaena. Opossum Hyaena.
*Lagunta, corinna, laoonana, ka-nunnah*

Dingo. Tasmanian Dingo. Panther.
Dog-Headed Pouched-Dog.
Pouched-Dog with Wolf Head.
*Lagunta, corinna, laoonana, ka-nunnah*

*Didelphis cynocephala* (1806),
*Thylacinus cynocephalus* (1824).
Excursion into sub-order *Dasyuromorphia*:
*Dasyurus cynocephalus* (1810),
from *dasyrus* meaning "shaggy tail".
*Lagunta, corinna, laoonana, ka-nunnah*

I've got you on the tip of my tongue.
You've got me under your skin.
Dog-Faced Dasyrus. Dog-Faced Opossum.
*Lagunta, corinna, laoonana, ka-nunnah*

48

Corinna could mean Brave. Corinna could be Fearless.
Wurrawanna Corinna, Great Ghost Tiger.
*Lagunta, corinna, laoonana, ka-nunnah*
*lowenin, cabbarrone-nenner, mannalargenna,*
*clinner, warternoonner, lartner, cannenner...*

SHOT

*Just off the Hobart wharves*
*I saw him sizing up his prey:*
*head stuck up upon a wall, shot*
*in silvered monochrome,*
*a photo in an internet café.*

*That pair of burning eyes,*
        *that famous wolfish grin:*
*another extinct Tasmanian,*
        *that damned smooth Errol Flynn.*

Just up the road, the Museum loops
        through enigmatic clips,
while this charismatic *loup garou*
        smacks predatory lips.

Errol left smooth talkies,
        but *our* star of silver screen
was more laconic Valentino:
        *that damned elusive thylacine!*

Errol's dad, the biologist
        Professor Thomas T. Flynn,
dreamed of a tiger sanctuary
        (though he also flogged their skins).

Now a pair of ghostly tigers
        guard Tassie's coat-of-arms,
as if heraldic thylacines
        could bark the next alarm.

Not rampant, couchant or dormant;
        nor *mordant* – for the dead don't bite –

those state-employed marsupials
    have long given up the fight.

*But if you listen closely,*
*to the creaking of your chair,*
*to the silence of your soul,*
*you can almost hear ghost tigers howl,*
*almost hear Trowenna moan.*

The last tiger in captivity
    died back in '36.
Though in the wild a few lived on
    with sighting in the sticks.

And half a century later,
    though officially extinct,
the odd backwoodsman claimed to see one,
    after a few big dead-stiff drinks.

When the Great Depression hit,
    the Zoo just couldn't cope,
the last tiger – one called Benjamin –
    well, there was never any hope.

And, although they called it Benjamin,
    seems God had done a switch:
the last thylacine was female,
    like Life, she was a bitch.

When the Head Curator died,
    his daughter Ali carried on;
fought to save the thylacine,
    though its time had come and gone.

Trained zoo staff were laid off,
    cheap "sussos" drafted in
– blokes working for their dole –
    while the system just caved in.

They evicted Alison Reid
    from her house inside the gates,
but still, unpaid, without a key,
    against economics and the State,

she cared for that last bloody thylacine.

The Zoo's last remaining carnivores,
    in the winter of '36,
were mangy, starveling creatures
    the sussos prodded at with sticks.

You could hear a pair of humbled lions,
    a Bengal tiger, the thylacine:
all howling in the snow, rain, sleet,
    while the wind scoured cages clean.

Benjamin died in Hobart
    in September '36,
two months after legislation
    to protect his/her species in the sticks.

They say that sometimes on that anniversary,
you can hear a distant howl.

*Could be in a bar in Hobart.*
*Could be drinking all alone.*
*Could be thylacine bitch or the jukebox,*
*leaking her soft hormonal moan.*

*Could be eavesdropping conversations.*
*Could be the chatter or the news.*
*Could be jaibird Pom or Vandemonian.*
*Could be the ancient Tassie Blues.*

(Heard tell that when he took
        that famous tiger footage,
the cameraman David Fleay
        took a nasty bite on the buttocks.)

*Just off the Hobart wharves*
*I saw him sizing up his prey:*
*a head stuck up upon a wall – shot*
*in silvered monochrome,*
*a photo in an internet café.*

*That pair of burning eyes*
*that famous wolfish grin:*
*another extinct Tasmanian,*
*that damned smooth Errol Flynn.*

# Devil

*Sarcophilus harrisii or Tasmanian devil*

### NIGHT ROAD

At night, your car lights catch a rowdy feast.
Chaotic, too anarchic for a *pack*. You watch
as they rip at road-kill. A strip of skin
wraps a thick neck like a stained napkin.
The carcass already unrecognisable,
but big enough for full-grown wallaby,
wombat. That mad scramble to get stuck in.

The harsh ecology of the road requires
a rigorous hygiene. These jaws need a verb
beyond *devour*: it's tireless work; machines,
mills grinding exceeding small. Waste disposal
units crunch right through decorum; strip, make *clean*;
render bones, clarify fat, recycle fur;
unglue the unholy mess your fender made,
your wheels stuck to this hopeless stretch of road.

All that and more: it is their gift to clear
that last bad bend right from your mind,
the blindness that threw its curved ball
of blood and bone, flesh and fear at your hasty night.
They make it go away. They make it disappear.

It's good to start each day afresh. New shift.
Clear the vermin from the place.
Friday, cock rifles, search out rats.

BLIND DATE

It's late. It's dark. Out back you catch
harsh coughs, a screech, something sharp
pitched between a challenge and a sneeze.

Beam blunts, greys this skinny bit of night,
then flits: white semaphors *belly*;
excited filaments, the whiskers' bright twitch.

Your flash lights up that famous mouth:
pink, staked with wide-spaced teeth;
red alerted ears burn by your torch,

the warm slant of back porch light.
(Times you've told the kids, ex-wife,
the stories on the phone, those ears could *ignite*.)

It's black, much smaller than you thought,
size of a piglet maybe: head quite big.
It stands its ground. You stare. It sniffs.

It's been the poltergeist in the barn;
its thing is rustle, rummage, felled rake,
ripped polythene, chewed boots.

Kept you awake nights, scratching
at the wood, screeching for a mate
(broadcast over the back few acres),

arranging for the odd blind-date.
And now, at last, you're in his face.
Something between you both – much more

than this lit-up overlapping slice of night.
You work this place; you drove the road
that dead-ends at the post-box on your gate.

Lost sight. He's gone, cold-shoulder;
slipped ears, flash, inside the night's black bag.
... You're left listening out.

Houseglow blunt on the fence. A few moths.
Dark presses that much colder to your face.

## DEVIL SANCTUARY

Glossy black, red tooth-snagged mouth,
Belial's party trick's to jump a branch,
rear up to sniff and snatch a chop
or freshly-hatcheted chicken leg
dangled from the keeper's fingers
– gingerly. "Good boy, Belial. Good boy."

"A devil's jaws give real bite-power,
strong as a dog's four times its weight.
Whiskers, long and lots of them:
good for foraging in the dark."
*Small lesions, lumps around the mouth,*
*soon tumours interfere with teeth.*

"Useful for dining etiquette
when communally ripping carrion.
Oh yes… At the devils' feasts,
whiskers measure space that's safe.
Let's them tuck in, get on with it,
beyond the range of another's bite."

"Good boy, Belial. Good boy."
*Studies show the cancer is transmitted*
*from mouth to mouth when devils bite*
*during aggressive mating or a fight.*

*Affected devils may have many*
*cancers throughout their bodies.*
*Check the dead or sick, but remember*
*battle-scarred or injured devils*
*or those with blood around their face*
*from feeding or from recent fights*
*could be mistaken as diseased.*

*Over periods of twelve to eighteen months*
*in high-density populations,*
*we now regularly see*
*up to one hundred percent mortality.*

EPITAPH
  *i.m. Sarcophilus harrisii.*

What's in a name? *Flesh-loving's* not enough;
*flesh-eating*, though, would be *sarcophagus.*

You're all jaw, teeth, gullet;
you work the world right through your gut.
          *Sarcophilus, sarcophilus,*
          a sarky grin and an oesophagus.

Memory coiled round your digestive tract,
you fillet history, chew on biology,
drop us these hard unpalatable little facts
and then you're gone with the morning dew.

All flesh, of course, is grass stepped on by us.
No chance. You got this cancer in your face:
bit off more than even you can chew,
else we would – *will* – wear your diet down to dust.

GRUNTS
*"Penguin Parade", Phillip Island, Victoria, Australia*

Sun's set
when the first's washed-up,
bewildered, on the shore.

Dark when another,
then another, peers to discover
they're on stage, and the set's a dim-lit planet:

*Astronauts* beamed down from twinkling infinities
navigated by star and starfish, the milky way of shoals,
crashing in through that last Van Allen belt of coast.

Or some strange salt-dazed foreign thing,
neither fish nor fowl: sleekness, a turn of speed,
swapped for the waddle of a baby with full nappy.

Tiny, the smallest species
– *Fairy Penguins* –
at the bottom of Victoria's garden.

Metaphors catch *us* not them:
in dark tiers, a blackened coliseum;
down there the *arena* still means "sand".

Tourists out from Melbourne for the day,
waiting, with soup and sandwiches, impatiently for the dark
while drivers smoke, coaches throb in the car-park.

The Visitors' Centre's a bunker
of mugs, keyrings, postcards, videos
starring the endangered charismatic elite.

On the shelf, by the darkening window,
acrylic cuddles overlook this useful, fox-haunted coast.
And now we're near enough to hush or prayer.

No cameras. *Just watch, be here. Be now,*
some gap-year backpacker whispers into his girlfriend's ear:
*what you get to take away, is what you learn to see.*

Parade? You see *Grunts*. One more platoon
hits the beach; begins the ragged struggle across the open rake,
up through sandhills, foxholes.

You hear the talk: check your watch.
Your coach is already revving beyond the stands.
You note your metaphors in your little plastic-covered book;

scurry over them along the boardwalk
with hundreds of your kind.

FOX

*Several European red foxes were illegally released in Tasmania in 2001*

I

This stuff and your mind's gone back to '98:
when one of many prowling Melbourne wharves
snuck aboard a container ship Burnie-bound.
Big news: whole state alerted, on the lookout:
*"Just hope that interloper's no pregnant bitch."*

Now, it's wild-life on the box, remote dropped,
slipped between the cushions, your fat backside.
When something happens it's like the channel hops,
splices in *Dad's Army* – "We're all doomed!"
Comic John Knox Scot meets Disney cartoon,
"Allow me to introduce Mr Fox." The villain's
a vulpine Terry Thomas: ancient quick-fire jokes.
*Why… Helloooo…* A catchphrase that mocks.
Off in the distance – *Boom Boom*!

II

Two kills already; show Doubting Thomases
credible sightings, evidence of carcasses;
elsewhere, *No shit, just check these scats.*

Taskforce: need trained foxhounds double quick,
unpack those dogs to sniff out that hot fox stink.
Urgent: sand-traps set to catch paw-prints;
rig infra-red up in the bush.

At night, our officers are out spotlighting,
looking to catch that gold eyeshine,

62

by which we mean that retinal reflection
that sorts the foxes from rabbits, feral cats,
all our usual home-grown marsupial stuff.

Let's hope those hounds can find,
say, a suckling vixen in her den;
get right in there, rip
mother, all her fox-cubs up.


III

At risk, this warm stuff that's got so rare
back on the big mainland: long-nosed potoroo,
southern and the eastern barred bandicoot,
spot tail, aka the tiger quoll,
tussock and the glossy grass skink.
Say nothing of the things you don't find elsewhere:
bettong, Tassie pademelon, eastern quoll.

As for our boy, that feisty little devil?
Well, we hoped he'd work the door:
bounce for our exclusive little club.
Tough out there these days. The forecast's poor.
All considered, it's looking grim.
Oh, yes, it's looking really crook
for everyone, especially him.

IV

Eradication's never worked.
Once established, forget shooting and baiting.
Back on Phillip Island, they're taking penguins:
small enough, one bite-sized snack to go.
What's left from eleven colonies not so long ago's
guarded by sharpshooters now.

Snipers in the sandhills: making sure
we still get to see the parade go by.


V

Bastard! Some hard-on in a combat jacket:
some bandoliered buzz-cut, snare-wire gun-freak
with a pocketful of pump-action freedom,
far-right amphetamines, disrupted pattern pamphlets,
laser-sighted bowie knife and long-term, short-wave pique…

They say some K-ration survivalist
brought in the cubs; bred the litters,
raised in fox-holes on trapped roo meat;
sat it out (*Puritabs*, waterproof matches,
leaf-litter thunderbox, winterized pup tent);
carefully planned each strategic release.

Back now, unbackpacked,
*Snugpack* 30 tog *Schlafsack* safely stowed;
cracking a cold one, thumb drumming the tinny;
catching the news;
oiling his pieces, testing the action;
marking the map, in his hardened den;
waiting for all hell to break
(Who? Who? Who the fuck did this?) loose.

# A NED KELLY HYMNAL

# Ned Kelly's Eyes

### I IMAGE

That's him, that awkward shadow, that black, that's Ned.
     He's painted out as if already dead.

Sometimes, it's just a blank, that slit for eyes.
     You look right through the man to clear blue skies.

Sometimes, that void's red-tinged with fire or dawn:
     the burbling billy-can, the day's first yawn.

Sometimes, the clouds in that gash blush with dusk:
     sky buries its burning cheek down in the dust.

Sometimes, there's a flash of silver, say sardines:
     that peeled-back strip you've keyed along the tin.

He has no eyes in the back of his head, of course.
     Sometimes, he rides away (*Black gun. Black horse.*)

into another picture. What's forged by smith
     from black's still fire-lit then, and riding into myth.

## II POSTER BOY

You've seen those Sidney Nolan paintings? Gawky
uniforms riding shotgun through red or ochre.
*Bush.* In the gums, a bucketed head: Ned's helmet,
that famous, awkward square of black. Wild whites,
eyes dotted, peepers trapped in its narrow slit.

I heard he did the first while on the run:
AWOL. Lying low. Military Police.
Those wartime letters, the Captain's uncracked morse
obliterating words and where you are.
Seems like the censor's ink has blacked Ned's face
or cut it out to hang on a WANTED poster.
It grows a beard while registers ping rewards,
show cash racked up in magnitudes of zeroes:
the price above that head dolorous with silver haloes.

III P.R.

Sydney 2000. Kellies by the dozens,
all got up like Sidney Nolan's trademark
black rectangles – stagey cloaks and guns –
bushrangers to fire-crack the Olympics open.

Dead, Ned's everywhere. There's no escape:
a man with a hundred shadows springing up.
A forger takes a dusty Nolan landscape,
blacks out a patch to get that masked man in,
then watches his newly inhabited scrub appreciate
faster than any downtown real estate.

An enigma in the painted bush
holds you, the viewer up. Under the hammer:
views to die for. Lock, stock and barrel.
A gavel shatters the panelled room's judicious hush.

Eyes peeled like hard-boiled eggs. Flecked red.
Yellow. Black-dotted. Jaundiced, downcast or lidded;
hooded with flame, day's end or blood.
Or pool-balls, yours, spotted, on the edge of the pocket:
one good crack (stripes, then on to the black)
and they're lined-up, potted.

Maybe that black, black square shows whites
so very white you think of a pair staring out,
framed by a cell-door's slit?

Or eyes you saw the day the constables rode in?
The Boss unhooked that length of rawhide
from behind the stable door...
*Whites*. And what peeped out from deep inside
that scared blackfella's skin.

V MUSIC HALL

Cracked twig. If what's next's not sudden racket,
then long silence. Retake that birdsong *da capo*.
Rosellas, lorikeets, kookaburras, trackers,
constables, galahs, sharpshooters, all beadily alert,
out there somewhere, sitting in the darkened pit.

Back in Melbourne, they're spilling beer. Cheers!
You're a pub ballad, you're a music hall song.
You listen out among the whistles, calls. That's it.
Centre-stage again, spot-lit: heart a metronome
ticking out long bars — doing time till it starts again.
They make a song and dance, aim to make you sing.

The ballad of your life lived out. Your song
– *A one-ah, a two-ah, a-three* – top of your lungs –
sung out among the crows and currawongs.

# A Ned Kelly Hymnal

I

> *Helmet or bucket?*
> *Kick it. Fuck it.*
> *What's it matter when*
> *eight thousand pounds*
> *press on four men's heads?*

Forget the Bible. Swords
beaten into ploughshares
are crook to what's hammered
out of duff ploughboards.

The twist that scragged
earth's arse got blunt;
now it's cheeky, bent
to a new job.

Helmet, chestplate:
riveted, rough
as rock-snagged half-acre,
but ready enough.

Hard to work the thick
plough-shares. Tested.
Proof to ten yards
with a Martini-Henry round.

Not quite what you'd expect?
A quarter inch of iron;
lappet hanging heavy
from its leather strap.

*Now constables come and go.*
*Down in Melbourne,*
*where the Yarra's too brown*
*to drink, too thin to plough,*
*the rumours grow.*


II

Memories of the Mollies:
our blacksmith's turned
seamstress; learned to sew
a dress of wild colonial iron.

*Vanity, vanity,* stitching rivets
through the bodice, lacing
glowing ribbons
through neck and sleeve.

No greave-plates, chain-mail,
gorget or visor.
They move heavy as iron-clads,
augur the tank.

Helmet or a bucket?
A veil of ore, bride's bonnet:
*travesty, travesty,*
that's married them to dark.

Inside it's loud and hot:
breath, beard rustling iron
against the blush
on each hidden cheek.

Four heavy morning suits
worn once only, at Glenrowan,
by Kelly, brother Dan,
Steve Hart and Joe Byrne.

*And who will sing the ballad*
*of the Hotel Glenrowan?*


III

Stopped at the Inn. Thin walls,
spinsters, Victorian wallpaper
pinned like a summer dress
to a mannequin.

Breastplate. Iron corset.
In the backroom,
a rifle's barrel
rests against a spindle.

Remember, some time back,
*a beard in a frock:*
*Steve, cross-dressed, saddling up,*
*spurs catching at his hem.*

And now the clumsy
groin-piece has gouged
a blackgum furrow
along a lacquered table.

Ninety-seven pounds
of imperturbability.
Each movement pondered,
in all its awful gravity.

Blinkered. Stare straight ahead.
That pull of earth.
Heaviness finding sweat
beneath the long oilskin coat.

It's not that heavy *Drizabone*
that's come unstitched,
but something closer worms
along your inner seams.

Some hidden thing unknits
the suit of bone, unskins,
turns inside out
the underthings of flesh.

Light through darkness,
could be Sunday coming in
like a bright silk sampler
on the walls of the Glenrowan.

> *No choirs yet, but organ stops,*
> *rumble, clacker of heels in aisles;*
> *knees hit boards; hymn books,*
> *hard-backed; pews creak. Begin.*

IV

They're banging in
great long nails of light,
might as well be outside,
see if those suits stand up.

Nowhere to run. No need to hide.
Shootout. Returning fire.

Shot and shot and shot, re-
load and shot and shot, re-

lentless trochees, spinning barrels,
heavy recoil and stink of cordite.
Slugs on flesh and ¡pang! on iron
as they take aim, go for legs.

Crossfire. *Blug!* is leg hit.
Joe Byrne killed.
Woodcrackle. Smokesmell.
Dan Kelly, Steve Hart dead

as hotel burns.
Flimsy underthings alight
and shining through its stays.
And Ned? And Ned?

Captured, they cut
the boot from his foot;
took it as a trophy
along with his Colt.

Hotel smoulders, locals
fossick for keepsakes:
spent cartridges, hooves
cut from their dead horses.

> *Filched from embers,*
> *something to remember them fellas by.*
>
> *Knot a square of wet linen*
> *around your nose and mouth.*
> *Smoke still stings your eyes,*
> *as bandannas turn sightseers bandits.*

*Laid out in whitestuff, shifts.*
*Spooked by sheets. Too late*
*for wound-dressers now.*


V

A photo of Kelly
the day before he's hanged,
shows he's casually arranged
a paralysed left arm:

hooked the dead meat
into his belt,
while his right's
nonchalant on his hip.

He's hip alright,
with a cool and oily quiff:
big-bearded prophet meets
an Elvis *avant la lettre.*

He stares the future out
– not going to fall
on his face or to his knees.
Glimpse some support

near the shackles
round Ned's ankles,
but it's still the eyes alright
that pull

that dead man upright,
to his feet,
free of all
that weight.

# Alternative Ending

*Sidney Nolan's Death of a Poet, Walker Art Gallery, Liverpool*

*Death of a Poet* was what they called it:
head hung in a branch; roughed-up paint;
wristy little vortices where rag
scrubbed board, twisted bark
right through flat mid-blue.
Bush. Heat-struck head hung
against a cloudless dumb forever.
Archaic. Stark.
               Not hard to see why
(a sniff of lemon leaves, a fierce Greek sky?)
the municipal Victorian neo-classical Walker
saw Orpheus. No lyre. Alternative ending:
his ripped silence after frenzied stalkers
had torn him limb from limb.
Forget downriver. There's no water;
here's what became of another *him*:
head tossed sky-high, caught in trees.

But what we've really got here's dead Ned's head.
So odd to find, in Liverpool,
his face for once – at last his naked skin.
Yet though he's out his box, escaped his tin,
and all around the bush is blasted through
to *ripolin* blue enamel skies
the one thing you can't see here is his eyes.

Tight shut. Not really him at all.
Death-mask or bust. Kicked the bucket.
Right now he's just something in the trees,
round as a gourd, shiny on top,
bald as baked clay, a terracotta pot.

Or one that's bloomed, blown, grown scratchy dry;
breeze-rustled beard ready to fall to scrub,
dead-headed by some passer-by.

# The Shoal Bay Death Spirit Dreaming

*After The Napperby Death Spirit Dreaming (1980): collaborative painting by Clifford Possum Tjapaltjarri (c. 1932-2002) and his brother Tim Leura Tjapaljarri (1929-1984).*

*i.m. Mark Leabeater (1955-2005).*

Somewhere between
the Mid-Winter Leaving Hobart Snooze
and the Mad Rush Nervous Sweat
Getting to the Airport Nightmare,
I fetch up in a Melbourne Museum
in front of *The Napperby Death Spirit Dreaming.*

I'm Cliff Forshaw, not Clifford Possum,
and, being somewhere between,
I haven't got a clue what this
(so far from surf, sea, shore)
or anything else, might mean.

But I'm thinking back, and I'm looking out,
if not exactly forward,
to the *any other business*
end of the itinerant's agenda.

The Arts Council warns that whites
have no rights to blackfellas' stories.
But what about a title? What about a name?
Don't we really all end up
in one of Dreamtime Cemetery's
seven basic plots?

Not even the Aborigines
have been here *ab origine*,
but came hunting in packs,
along with the sniff of man's best friend.

Among the kookaburras,
the flash of rosellas,
these poems may contain images
of deceased whitefellas.


¶


*Ultimo in Arvo,*
sounds like a Latin motto.
But it's just a black and white photo
of a Sydney street, some spot near Darling Harbour,
on a sunstruck afternoon.

And it's endless now, what's burned in light:
sun, afternoon, the shadows
never quite making it to evening,
to the terminus and the cool rattle
of the last train home.


¶


Sun-worship: bodies
felled on the beach, each stripped right
down to tan, grin, teeth.


¶


The sun has slipped dark coins
under so many skins,
left obols on a country's tongue.
And now the state's left wondering
if it's enough to pay their way
to the other side of surf.

Out there, outlined against the crashing light,
a dark figure barely on that board
hangs ten.


¶


Its vegetable love will grow:
rhizomes, tubers,
sprout right through

gonna take some rake
to sort your nitty-gritty,
dig up them bulbs,
their harsh night-glow

gallow's laughter,
keep your humour,
say the word,
(it's in the timing)
say it, say it: *tumour.*


¶


Upon a man in black
with a cracked voice
I seemed to have stumbled.
"How's it goin', Lenny Cohen?"
"Mustn't grumble,"
I heard him mumble.


¶

Mark pops pills – in a flash Max is back
devouring what they gave his daylight twin,
for when it all gets too much.

A little bit of R & R
at pharmacology's cutting edge.
Hanging with the guys,
might as well blunt the day with a dry run,
as sun pours itself another,
the doctor lies down to his siesta,
and Mr Hyde foams up to beer o'clock.

Be time enough back in Sydney,
to steel the mind, clench the sphincter,
then do the only thing you can really do:
lie back, relax, let white stuff go soft,
fold innocent as butter, melt
around the knife of burning light.


¶


*Palliative*:
To lessen the severity of (pain, disease etc)
without curing or removing;
to seem less serious by concealing evidence;
from *pallium*, Latin for "a cloak",
which is also a word for the cerebral cortex
and contiguous white matter.

Out in the night, drunken nutters:
neighbours, all that contiguous white matter.


¶

From Zenith to Wreck
(the way they name these beaches).
Blue moon. No, really.
And the sound of surf
sweeping grit along the bay.

The evening's polarised
to blue and gold, or peeling away
between sky-scuds and sea-caps.

That day, we forded water to the spit,
rucksack above head,
trying not to get the camera wet.
Glad now to have those photographs,
the notebook which says we saw,
at the end of their season,
a pod of humpbacks heading north;
ate barramundi and kangaroo pies;
lost count of skydivers piling into blue;
heard you say:
"Every time I look up into the sky,
there's someone falling out."


¶


Unignorable horn. Man
slumped over the steering wheel
of a beat-up van.
Raid on the inarticulate;
his shabby equipment
deteriorated far enough:
*Please Clean Me!*
wet-fingered in the dust.

¶

Through painful sun,
near Carthage, years ago,
I saw a cellarful of sarcophagi,
names cut into stone in
(am I right in thinking) *Greek*?
(am I right in thinking *Carthage*?)

Sometimes the chiseller,
starting with too generous a space,
had not anticipated the stone's edge
and, running out of tomb,
had to cramp or abbreviate forever,
docked the last recorded syllables
of a loved, hated or feared one's name.

As much as I remember: long time ago
with a woman whose passport once bore,
next to *next-of-kin*, the curt formula
of my initials, surname, the country where I lived.


¶

Heard your last trip was to the outback.
Never made it myself to the Red Centre,
just flew over its dusty suburbs.

Hope that where you find yourself, there's
no spider in the dunny, snake across your path.
Well, what's the chance of something lethal now?
Or do we still forever need to do the maths?

¶

Here is seven yards and more of Dreaming
and other Dreamings bracketed within
its slow pan across the Western Desert:
Old Man's Dreaming, Yam Dreaming,
Sun and Moon Dreaming.

Here is acrylic psychogeography,
brain-pan soup, palimpsest of soul,
mind's hypertext.

A field of dots may mask the sacred, keep it secret.
The point of pointillism's what's between:
something scanned and reconstituted
behind the eyes and in-between
the buzz of hertz.

*Students will read stories of the Dreaming
and discuss ownership of these stories.
They will view an Aboriginal artwork
and identify meaningful signs and symbols.
Students will also write a short story
about their own spiritual beliefs, land and family
and create a painting to describe this story.*

# Notes

Two books in particular provided many of the historical details incorporated into these poems: *The Fatal Shore* by Robert Hughes (Collins Harvill, 1987) and *Thylacine* by David Owen (Allen and Unwin, 2003). I would like to thank their authors for their invaluable research and insights.

p. 9 *Vandemonian*: Sir George Arthur was appointed Lieutenant Governor of Van Diemen's Land in 1823. Arthur organized the Black Line fiasco, which was intended to drive the Aborigines into the Tasman Peninsula where they could be controlled. He founded Port Arthur as a prison settlement for deported convicts on a further peninsula connected by a narrow isthmus, guarded by dogs (The Dog Line) at Eagle Hawk Neck Bay, to the Tasman Peninsula itself. The quatrain beginning "The very day we landed upon the fatal shore" (p. 14) is a traditional song.

p. 23 *Trucanini*: Trucanini, the last of the full-blood Tasmanian Aborigines, was born on Bruny Island around 1812. After many of her family and tribe were killed or sold into slavery she joined builder-turned-evangelist George Augustus Robinson and his guide the Aboriginal chief Woorady on his journeys of exploration and "conciliation." During the early 1830s Robinson made contact with every remaining group of Tasmanian natives and carried out rudimentary anthropological inquiries into their customs and rituals, as well as compiling basic vocabularies of their languages. (The poem 'Thylacinus Cynocephalus', p. 48, utilises one of his word-lists of thylacine names). After the failure of The Black Line (1829) to pen the Aborigines in the Tasman Peninsula, in 1834 Robinson led the remaining natives to Flinders Island in the Bass Strait, where he attempted to Christianize them. The "National Picture" showing Robinson and Trucanini "bringing in" the remaining Aborigines is Benjamin Duttereau's *The Conciliation* (1840). By 1845 there were 150 Aborigines left. Robinson had left Flin-

87

ders to return to the mainland in 1839; his successors treated the remaining aborigines in their concentration camp appallingly. In 1846 the survivors were settled at Oyster Cove on the D'Entrecasteaux Channel near Hobart where their keepers provided them with insanitary huts and rum. By 1855 there were only sixteen left, including Trucanini. The last man, William Lanne, died in 1869. Trucanini died in 1876.

There is of course a big problem about the concept of "the last of the Aborigines"; many Tasmanians are mixed-race descendents of Aborigines and immigrants.

p. 39 *Tiger*: The Van Diemen's Land Co. introduced a bounty in 1830; in 1888 the Tasmanian Parliament placed a price of £1 on the thylacine's head. The last thylacine was captured and sold to Hobart Zoo in 1933. The last captive thylacine died in Hobart Zoo in 1936, the same year it was added to the list of protected wildlife. The Tasmanian tiger was declared extinct by international standards in 1986.

p. 48 *Thylacinus Cynocephalus*: In *The Last Tasmanian Tiger*, Robert Paddle points out that the common but incorrect translation as "the dog-headed pouched-dog" is both inelegant and "borders upon the stupid and crass."

p. 62 *Fox*: The fox poses a huge threat to native Australian fauna, having caused the decline and extinction of many native species on the mainland, where where may be up to 30 million foxes. The fox's absence has allowed Tasmania to become something of a Noah's Ark for Australian animals. Foxes were first introduced to Australia in the 1850s by wealthy settlers who wanted to hunt them on horseback.

p. 77, *The Shoal Bay Death Spirit Dreaming*: 'The Napperby Death Spirit Dreaming' (1980) is a collaborative painting by Clifford Possum Tjapaltjarri (c.1932-2002) and his brother Tim Leura Tjapaltjarri (1929-1984).

# Biographical Note

CLIFF FORSHAW left school at sixteen and worked in an abattoir before studying painting at art college and developing an interest in languages and European literatures. After various jobs in Spain, Mexico, Italy, Germany and New York and freelance writing in London, he completed a doctorate on Elizabethan satire at Oxford. Since then he has lived in Snowdonia and Yorkshire and taught at Bangor, Sheffield and, since 2005, Hull University.

He has been a writer-in-residence in California, Transylvania and Tasmania, twice a Hawthornden Writing Fellow, and a winner of the Welsh *Academi* John Tripp Award. He continues to paint and his work has been exhibited in the UK and USA. He has also made two short films to accompany poetry collaborations: *Drift* was shown at the Humber Mouth Literature Festival in 2008; *Under Travelling Skies* (Kingston Press, 2012) won the first Larkin 25 Words Award in 2012.

Cliff Forshaw also writes fiction.